Turtle Beach

Explorer Challenge

Find out what happens
to this shell …

OXFORD
UNIVERSITY PRESS

Floppy was barking at something in the back garden.
"What is it?" asked Kipper.
"Look!" said Biff excitedly. "It's a hedgehog!"
Mum told Floppy to get back in the house. "I like hedgehogs," she said. "They're good for the garden."

The children watched the hedgehog move slowly along the bottom of the fence.

"I don't think it wants to stay in our garden," said Chip. "It looks as if it's trying to get into next door's garden."

The hedgehog disappeared under a bush next to the shed. The children waited for it, but it didn't come out.

"I hope it's OK," said Kipper as they all went inside. "What if it was trying to find its way home?"

In Biff's room later, the children were reading about hedgehogs in an animal book. They were still talking about them when the key began to glow.

"We're off on another adventure!" said Biff, grabbing the key.

The key took them to a beautiful, sandy beach on a moonlit night. They could hear the sound of the waves.

Kipper saw something further up the beach. There was a large, dark shape on the sand. "What's that?" he asked.

"Let's investigate!" said Biff.

When they got closer, Chip said, "Wow! It's a huge sea turtle!"

An older girl was sitting nearby. "Please don't get too close," she whispered to the children.

The turtle was pushing sand into a hole with its back flippers.

"Why is it doing that?" asked Kipper quietly.

This turtle came ashore to lay her eggs," the girl explained. "Now she's covering them up."

"How long has she been here?" asked Biff.

"I spotted her about twenty minutes ago," said the girl, frowning.

"What's the matter?" asked Chip.

Turtles usually come back to the same beach every year to lay their eggs," the girl said, "but some of our beaches have changed a lot recently."

"How?" asked Biff.

The girl gestured towards a building further down the beach. "There's a new hotel," she said.

When all the eggs in the hole were covered with sand,
the turtle began to turn slowly around using her flippers.

"What's she doing now?" asked Chip.

"She needs to get back to the sea," said the girl.

Just then, a cloud crossed the moon.

The children watched as the turtle began to crawl along the beach.

"Oh dear," the girl said. "I think she's a bit confused. She isn't going straight down the beach towards the sea. Look! She's heading towards that new boat ramp."

The turtle paused near the boat ramp. Then she
turned and slowly crawled up the beach.

"She's going away from the sea now!" said Chip.

"Oh no!" said the girl. "She must think the light from
the hotel is moonlight on the water! She thinks she's
heading for the sea!"

"Maybe we can turn her around so she's going the right way," suggested Biff.

The girl shook her head. "No chance," she said. "These turtles are much too heavy for that."

The turtle continued to crawl slowly up the beach.

The girl looked worried. "At the top of the beach there's a steep slope down to the road," she said. "If she falls down that, she'll never be able to pull herself out!"

"I've got an idea," said Biff, "but we'll need to get help from the hotel."

"I'll come with you," said the girl. "My uncle's a
wildlife ranger – I'll call him and explain everything.
Come on!"

"What should *we* do?" asked Kipper.

"Just try to keep an eye on the turtle," said Biff.
Biff and the girl ran off.

At the hotel, the girl ran to telephone her uncle.
Biff ran up to the front desk and explained the
problem. "The turtle's moving towards the light from
the hotel, so can you turn all the lights off, please?"
she said.

The man behind the desk shook his head. "I'll have to ask the manager about that," he said.

"There isn't enough time!" said Biff. "We have to save the turtle."

Two hotel guests were passing by and overheard. "Quick," a woman said. "Do what this girl says!"

On the beach, Chip and Kipper did not know what to do. They could only watch as the turtle continued pulling herself closer and closer to the slope.

"Where's Biff?" asked Kipper nervously.

Suddenly everything went dark as all the hotel lights went off.

A minute later, the boys saw the flash of a torch. Biff and the girl were back!

"My uncle will be here as soon as he can," said the girl.

"And the hotel staff lent us this torch," said Biff. "I want to try something!"

Biff moved down the beach, shining the torch back and forth on the sand.

"If the turtle mistook the hotel lights for moonlight, maybe she'll think my torchlight is the moon!" she said.

For a long time, however, the turtle did nothing.

Then, very slowly, she began to turn round.

"I think it's working!" said Kipper. "She's turning the right way again!"

Just then, the light from the torch began to fade.

"Oh no! The battery must be running out!" said Biff.

"What now?" said Kipper.

The exhausted turtle was no longer moving. The children watched her helplessly. Some of the guests from the hotel were watching, too. Nobody knew what to do.

Suddenly, the thick clouds that had covered the moon moved away.

The bright light of the full moon shone down on the beach again. Its reflection sparkled on the water.

The children held their breath and waited.

After a while, the turtle began to move again. It was clear she was very tired.

"Come on," said Chip. "You can do it!"

The turtle had reached wet sand.

"Not far to go," said Biff.

At last the turtle came to the first gentle wave. Then she slipped into the dark water.

"She's made it!" said Kipper.

From further up the beach, the hotel guests cheered.

The girl's uncle was watching, too.

"I got here as soon as I could," he explained, "but it looks as though you didn't need my help. Well done, children!"

"What about the baby turtles?" asked Kipper. "Will they be OK when they hatch from the eggs?"

we'll mark the nest," said the ranger. "It's easy for baby turtles to go in the wrong direction, so we'll watch out for when they hatch."

"And we can turn the hotel lights out again when that happens," said the hotel manager, who had joined them on the beach.

The girl turned to Biff. "Thank you so much for everything," she said.

"You're welcome," said Biff. "I'm really glad we could help."

The key was glowing in Biff's hand. It was time for the children to go home.

Back at home, Kipper ran to find Dad.

"I've had an idea to help the hedgehog!" he said. "What if we made a hole in the fence?"

"I was just talking to our neighbour about that," Dad said. "She said people can make hedgehog highways. Hedgehogs use them to go from garden to garden."

The next day, Mum and Dad cut a small hole in the fence. As it got dark, the children waited. Finally a little dark shape emerged from the bush. The hedgehog! It disappeared through the hole.

Dad smiled. "Now there's nothing stopping you three from going where you need to be," he told the children. "Bed!"

Retell the Story

Look at the pictures and retell the story in your own words.

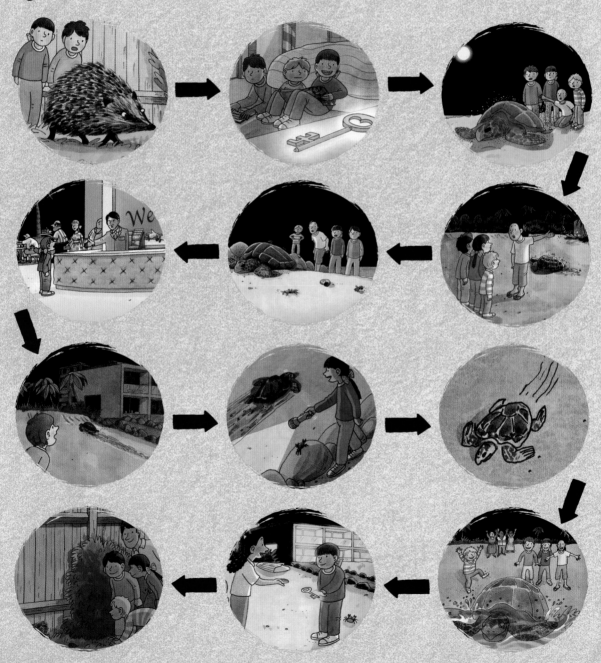

Look Back, Explorers

Where was the hedgehog trying to go?

What words can you think of to describe how the turtle moved?

What did Biff ask the hotel to do?

What happened to the turtle in the story? Can you explain where she went and why?

Why does the hotel manager say they can turn out the hotel lights when the baby turtles hatch?

Did you find out what happened to this shell?

What's Next, Explorers?

Now you've read about a turtle finding its way back to the sea, find out about habitats where other animals live ...

Rock Pool to Rainforest

Anita Ganeri
Series created by Roderick Hunt and Alex Brychta

OXFORD

Explorer Challenge
for *Rock Pool to Rainforest*

Find out how this animal keeps cool ...